FRANCESCO PRIMERANO

120 years of Cinema
by Lumière broters in 50 shades of grey

Youcanprint *Self-Publishing*

Titolo | 120 Years of Cinema by Lumière brotes in 50 shades of grey
Autore | Francesco Primerano
ISBN | 978-88-93065-49-8

Youcanprint Self-Publishing
Via Roma, 73 – 73039 Tricase (LE) – Italy
www.youcanprint.it
info@youcanprint.it
Facebook: facebook.com/youcanprint.it
Twitter: twitter.com/youcanprintit

The notes and pages of 120 years of cinema, colors more 'variety, shapes and content more inviting, open, they browse, read, scrutinize, they love and then close with the hope and the desire to read them again with the same passion that he had initially presented.

Francesco Primerano

Cinema, in the heyday of its first 120 years of life

A Sophia Loren and Brigitte Bardot, the stunning 2 octogenarians who lit the cinema world in the best way

A Marilyn Monroe, to more than 50 years after his mysterious disappearance

A James Dean, 60 years after his tragic death

The great absent: Totò, Grace Kelly, Paul Newman, Marlon Brando, Steve McQueen, Marcello Mastroianni, Anna Magnani, Mariangela Spalato, Virna Lisi, Robin Williams, Paul Walker
and many others ......

TABLE OF CONTENTS

PRODUCTION
DIRECTOR
CAMERA
DATE   SCENE   TAKE

INTRODUCTION
120 years of cinema

It is an attractive and compelling, cinematic story, known by all as the great ideas factory. The history of cinema is presented as a planetary firmament of myths and actors as timeless and ineffable and sublime art form. Each historical period is flourishing and overtime to film the show, where everything, even the most trivial, expresses its peak. The film, in any kind is present, the show is ideal where it captures the supremacy of the soul, where the glory is the result of ideas and interpretations, where the style is unmistakable and emotions come to life in an unprecedented virtuosity . The book in question simply wants to celebrate 120 years of Cinema, the same cinema that made us love, dream and paint the best nectars of our lives, making us understand that despite everything, the show must go on. It is a journey into the world of cinema, the first short story "The arrival of a train at La Ciotat" (1895) by the Lumière brothers to the current movie "50 shades of gray" by Sam Taylor-Johnson, between 1000 timeless myths, from Marilyn Monroe to Audrey Hepburn, Marlon Brando James Dean, from Sophia Loren to Gina Lollobrigida, Totò, Massimo Troisi, Elizabeth Taylor and Brigitte Bardot, from Monica Vitti in Virna Lisi, Alberto Sordi Roberto Benigni.

FIRST CHAPTER

The magical films of world cinema

The year was 1895, when the Lumière brothers put on film the scene of the train entering the station of La Ciotat. That historical frame is the start of a wonderful adventure called Cinema, which today celebrates with great pleasure and vigor, its first 120 years of glorious existence. Cinema is the place where you can keep a dynamism lived in all its wonders and where scenes can be shot in an exemplary manner, if everything can go smoothly along the paths of the heart and the soul. You can see the vitality of the people who build and destroy their myths in the space of a morning or even in a few hours. There are those who turn a huge amount of films getting a public success triumphant and who loses in the arduous path sets the most difficult and hostile. Some films take on the dark tones and dramatic and certain characters are captured in their twisted personality and observed by the watchful eye of the director. There are interpreters of musical comedies that find their way into parts of great value and the various flavors of world cinema. There are successful writers who can create texts that are worth their extraordinarily brilliant Oscar nomination and there are others that come out permanently from that environment. There are films that have positive results around the world and find them even in art cinemas and nightclubs in the various schedules, like those directed by Federico Fellini and Luchino Visconti. The complaints are positive and attractive when everything is ingenious in representing the life of every day and in all the scenes narrated by the soul. The objects used in movies are always original and revolutionary flames for the sake and pleasure of all. There are people influenced by other directors and sometimes the impressionist style gets the better of everything, absolutely everything. In the masterpieces of always captures the rose on the streets and on the rails of the soul, there are fears for his life but rejoices for the adventures imprinted in timeless images. There are those who represent the essence and who plays only the appearance, who teaches how to move in complicated scenes and wild and who finds comfort and peace in territories peacefully without being flooded with 1000 issues. There are artists who go beyond the limits with their own ideas in a crescendo of symphonic sounds newspapers; They call those sounds and the image responds in challenging styles and types of different themes. The taste of life and the taste of daily life, subjects rejected by society, the moving interpretation of some characters and the stories of various prejudices are the themes most appreciated by the public and the trademark of many studios. Everything becomes impenetrable and seems to float on the desire to make it more difficult roads of Cinema. The phone rings and anything goes in dramas of success, bringing out the eyes of many characters oblivion of an endless road. The different sets you can see passionate embrace between lovers, some unripe love, stories from fellow Jews and simian in appearance of good people. The films make good consumerism of years: moving scenes in difficult times fragile, the underwater worlds from nothingness of appearance affect the time that slide between notes happy soul, stories of American life take over of silly comic scenes of trivial, the charm and the enigma win on platitudes and arrogance, the musical quickly became the most popular film by the people it's worth, the gangsters and the horror are other genres that go great among boys of all ages and western affecting more and more fans more demanding.

Steven Spielberg and Oliver Stone are among the most beloved film of all time among the supporters of the genre. In some societies the idealistic slogans fundamental for life become the subjects discussed in the Cinema, which are clear and sharp differences among people and where no longer remembers the law. The play assumes a spectacular in the film business since the early years of the 900, where everything seems natural and fast, where the beats fast and straightforward prevail over the rest. Victims of the imagination of others reach a new combination of realism: are felt francs tones and sharp people now destroyed by the judgments of others, you can see the biggest optimist and who looks at life in a bitter vision tremendously. There are those who want to represent the complexity of the lives of people in despair and who wants to describe the subject fascinated by social patterns to follow. Also you see the dancing lights and shadows in fantastic scenarios, the humiliations of those who surrender to the evidence of failure and criticism of those social mixes with stylized images. And in one of the most innovative of the Cinema you can see the poignant story of humanity recounted, step by step, by the greatest of the century as Federico Fellini, Bernardo Bertolucci, Mario Monicelli, Antonioni Giancarlo and Luigi Comencini. Among a number of clippings and flickering funny, it creates a movement of souls in the party with new characters that can attract the public. There are events traditionalist and modern stories told over the years. Also transcribed glimpsed images of wallpaper stained with techniques and messages of affection, ideas and actions are perceived in constant boil and live adventures that extend the stories of young artists on wonderful roads of glory.

CINEMA

SECOND CHAPTER

Souls Film smiling at life

The environment is affected by film appearances spectacular and timeless, where you play with sound and where innovation is ingenious made possible only thanks to the music. There are pictures and stories that inspire maneuvers film between tenderness and humor, where the continuity of the scenarios has a soft and attractive visual beauty out of control. The plots are shown in the most joyful and fascinated human beings who open themselves to life. All this and more is the industry of Cinema: there are lights that illuminate the darkness and inscrutable faces of people in search of an author. The atmosphere as the best beauty, thanks to masterful directors such as Ettore Scola, Roberto Rossellini, Dino Risi, Federico

Fellini, Bernardo Bertolucci, Mario Monicelli, Luchino Visconti and there are images that evoke worlds in scented entire fields of happiness. Lost lovers and witnesses of tragic events, beautiful love stories, nostalgia for a time lived, the mirror of our world, are some topics that are recounted in grand style with timeless film. You may notice the strong characters, spensieratezze enveloping and passions common among young actors: those who evade the realistic visions of life, who feels a sense of humanity in everything he does and who simply enters the world of illusions. For some, the game rule is to distinguish the good from the curses of unscrupulous people. Alfred Hitchcock, the largest maker of images of the century, by which all are enchanted, has established itself in the world of cinema thriller and beyond. Brilliant movie where we want to prove the unprovable and knowledge of the fear that is in the newspaper have been the focus of criticism and magical experiences. See photos and pictures which show that the shock is coming and that the details are used as exclamation points to the story of a broken life. The children of the sky, the lies peddled by some people unnamed, exaggerations without control, the central ambitions of young talent, the strong desires to escape, the poetry of the dialogue, the story pleasant taste, are other topics that are covered in the several prestigious films. The figures of actors and screen idols, the accurate filmographies who enjoyed a long of public favor, the stimulating experiences of young people in action, the fond memories of good people, representing some stages of film history and to see the ' together we are located in the heart of many photographs without history. Wherever emerges the challenge of commercial films more exciting and imported all over the world to win souls purer and thinking.

CHAPTER THREE

Cinema between 1000 Dreams and Myths

Evocative ambience and natural light flooding the floors of a magic never seen before, the magic of cinema. The minds of the people are abducted from attractive and compelling stories: someone takes the shadows of other directors and who is inspired by the next to tell the pages of madness, of wonder and fantasy. Some people collect the atmosphere of dreams, who enacts stories visually stronger than others and who tells the adventures of eternal boys and buxom maidens. There are brilliant images of funny people who are reconciled with the thrilling scenes, joys found that become tragedies, romantic stories that turn into dramatic scenes, the freedom experienced in some corners of the sky, set gigantic city and wonderful trails below a scorching sun in mid-August. They glimpsed in the human images of a child with so many hopes and dreams of all kinds, fashions shared between people of different races and between rebels, the good and the curses of all kinds. There are clouds that pass in front of the moon movie: free association of divine pleasure, unconscious mechanisms that cross the kindest souls, boxes of desires and thoughts of 1000, fears of sex, fittings scenes of other times, visions of interesting stories, poisons sweetened by the presence of valorous people. The forms used are the same as ever and represent the milestones of artists that have forever changed the history of world cinema !? Cinema as "Seventh Art" is stronger than any other event, according to many critics and experts from different sectors, because in it we explore the various steps of the life as a real stage where everything counts, even the superfluous. Ballets traditional rooms conventional terrifying moments, strange shots, montages of emotion and amazement of the best ways, are other examples and testimonies of cinema that we try to live, upsetting all the spectators. There are those who takes scenes that justify violence and who rapes his own soul by defeating the desire to love and to dream. In the movie is taken by all: women motionless in the sun, soldiers killed but smiling, with beauty and charm, the fashions of all time and for all budgets, pictures of pretty girls in oasis of eternal magic. In all this there is always the director who knows how to provoke deep emotions in the audience through scenes unforgettable masterpieces that have left their mark and movie noble and brave.

FOURTH CHAPTER

The magical journey
into the world of cinema

It is taking place around the world in several successful films, where everything is built of coral islands: the indispensable basis for the development of the film is also the soul of the actors and of all that is around. Retracing roads and trails of all kinds: nightlife outlying towns, young people bewitched by the beauty of life that they forget the problems and business of all kinds, distribution of advertising signboards sacrificed between a signal and the other. All inspired by the daily life to suit the tastes of everyone and to satisfy the public in its fullness. You can see the magic of some scenes to gain success and to find the secret of happiness. The tale of surreal stories and incredible on the roads of the soul and purity of women, represent the last stop granted to a mysterious land of illusion to stop thinking so time. And then sprouting Totò, Laurel and Onlio, Charlie Chaplin, Alberto Sordi, Roberto Benigni, Ugo Tognazzi, Paolo Villaggio and Massimo Troisi, who bring laughter to power with their genius in their hilarious comedy shows, places where clean and crystalline are the their soul in the endless seas of lightheartedness. The real purpose is to make people laugh and have fun for a lot of artists: those who believe in their quality and who wonders on the obscure future. In many scenes you can find the true meaning of movie characters that made history: who reads for the sake of acting and those who do it for the success ruthless. Remember historical interpretations and brilliant actors like Gregory Peck, Gary Cooper, Paul Newman, Sean Connery, Marlon Brando, that remain etched in the minds of each of us: there are those who feel much the film and the character he plays and who He reviewed in his unfortunate appearance by scemotto duty. There are those who savor the criticisms and enticements that are always nice to the great talents of the cinema and who finds a great way to make life better people. Clarity and joy of souls in celebration of the masterpieces of all time, flowing living and tenacious in the world spectacular and attractive is the Cinema. There are as talented, stunning spells and many surprises to discover, through the blood of people who have left their mark in the history of world cinema. The contrast between the precursors and pioneers of comedy horror author, there is often traveling to those vehicles of well-being and great humility that are important for the success of a film. In spells film of all time, you can also notice documentaries on the everyday life of people of great human. There are masterpieces that spring topped the charts of the most popular films, where strong histrionic personality and versatile forward immediate emotions that everyone can use and where peace and stability in the most prestigious roles in shows ever harbored. Protagonists of a series of successful films compete to do anything and dress every role that is congenial to their true nature. Open spaces in the city are described in enchanting dream movie: who has a predilection for the refinements and who has the best taste in the details, those involved and those meticulous chronicle of fantastic transformations. There are people desperate and helpless that remain etched in the memory of the viewer, and you can feel the approaches to the cinematic stories dream and the lives of those copyrights.

FIFTH CHAPTER

What a great show that is the Cinema

The movie-poster of our society and our future present themselves in their best shows of all time: from adventurous to those fantastic scenes, compelling stories from those magical stories from real ones out of time. There are themes and interesting subjects that are addressed in films with great depth: the gray dawn that rises on a green hill, a great awakening among all lovers of the world, our pockets full of things to say, good jokes for lucky star, a ray of sunshine in the wheel of life. To this you can add the brightness that comes anywhere and take the best days, dancing out of the ocean. In these films they are narrated feelings of freedom, happiness and lives of flavors visceral. In them you live in the real values of a life always inviting, where wild horses run along the streets of the soul. Inside the boundary of each man they are perceived deeds and misdeeds of unforgettable stories: who dries the stars from the eyes of a dream to be realized or can love and who lets the sun fall on good people. It is displaced by the advent of high-level star and beautiful women and charming, praising the best artists in the world. You may remember the legendary Marilyn Monroe, sexy symbol of the 50s', fabulous sign of seduction and set of vulnerabilities: the biggest movie star ever existed, with a desire to survive and emerge. Our queen set proves always radiant, and also the extraordinary openness and the wide availability make it the simple girl next door (the anti-diva par excellence). Eternal enchantress with her provocative optimism continues to hold on us, 50 years after his death, proving much more than a sex symbol. On the streets of the various film sets you live and perceive events and attractive streets by having to spread: the description of dramatic stories of each value and of great social impact, an odyssey of facts and pleasures to tell and to show off, racing moved to the success and to the vanity of life, the details of a youth a little 'faded but always present, beauty care and in detail, the trouble of thinking and more. All this happens in the fabulous world of cinema, of our dear friend and Cinema. The Light Room opens in new artists and new talents, following the sun of their thoughts and their small and big ideas. Amazing results, extraordinary effects never seen come to life again as scenarios of the past. Those who want to escape from the reality of things, those who simply want to play with our erotic imagination, who takes wonderful performances and those who paint tinted windows. The inventions of our existence flood the face of the soul and the illusions of our being furtive move towards new horizons. Glimpse dark rooms where the wheel turns and the light in the minds of people of great value, you live impressions of all kinds and you notice cameras colorful and full of vitality. In film thickness, light filters and projects, in a sublime way, the magic of the biggest movie stars like Paul Newman, Cary Grant, Marlon Brando, Greta Garbo, Ingrid Bergman and Gregory Peck. You can also breathe the shock of the news and you can live and perceive scenes of yesteryear. The first magical touches Film can be tasted with directors of special effects and timeless images, with lights of distant stars that cover the tracks of life.

SIXTH CHAPTER

The fabulous world of Cinema

Cinema is followed like a beacon that illuminates the finest minds and among its pioneers you can see a gallery of actors and stars of all time, John Wayne, Robert De Niro, Anna Magnani, Marilyn Monroe, Elizabeth Taylor, Sophia Loren, Gina Lollobrigida, Catherine Deneuve and Alain Delon. You can breathe a variety of cinematic elements: colored lights of the cosmos, body experiences, excellent close-ups, details of carefree people and a language of ideas and hopes that illuminate the paths of great humanity. So you can taste the true meaning of life, the eternal magic shows and still images and reflected on mirrors or rotating inside a colored box. S'intravedono cities rich in fantasies, using films and rollers that make a film something extraordinary, are perceived characteristics of particular individuals who demonstrate the best of their charm, they will discover the best qualities and the sincerity of the most tangible and gestures We appreciate the larger aspirations of every individual. The lives of some actors run placid, hoping to appear more lives of others that seemed to die into nothingness. They see brains on fire and lived successes that generate other successes. The World Film revolves around not only in Rome, but also to all the best places ever. In the highlights and shadows of the metropolis you will live unforgettable interpretations, points and main aspects of the film that made an epoch. They build the true portraits of great value and movies analyze the path of young people to knowledge and truth. Other scenes are shot on a minimal budget: someone tells lives marked by adventures and dramatic stories and who wants to be out of time and 1000 spaces of memory. You see stories of lives worth living to the end, tell an Italian weddings and divorces of international flavors, tragedies of those too young to die, curses and so many lives to be saved, the young rebel in search of easy success and carefree , shady characters, violent and unfriendly. The actors seem to live for their work!? Who ferociously pursues success and who has specific plans to get it if it kills me. They tell also lives without purpose and causal and simply those who remember Peter Pan, as he popped up from the island that is not there and we had to stay.

CHAPTER SEVEN

1000 shades of Cinema

The world of cinema presents us with a number of memorable characters and figures that fill the film with big ideas of humanity and strength of mind, with careers marked by appearances bulky and sudden disappearances: Monica Vitti, Lucia Bosè, Anna Magnani, Sophia Loren, Virna Lisi. With savage irony of the final and with various twists we are often on the trail of the essential elements of historical films and high-impact, where the fatal passions unite the protagonists, reducing them to realize the superior design of their lives. We are facing a Cinema that combines the secrets of success and adventure more true: there are rich cast of stars and old stars and some people have the habit of confessing his nightmares and his torture. Loves of a sad girl airhead, angels abandoned in the middle of a road, the film posters from different periods, are at the center of all that can serve to a movie to emerge. It saw the birth of prestigious actors and setting, defining popular and modern aspects of the collective, they live symphony of colors that plunge from the sublime scenes of a movie and everyone is laid bare. Great adventures ranging in fields more or less profound: the strong illusions of young hopefuls, the average American man movie, surveys on women and on subjects of great luxury in search of an author. The concentration of the film transports the viewer into a whirlwind ever closer through a series of events of the day and night euphoria youth. Note the syndrome perverse actor who wants to look at all costs, there are people with strengths and weaknesses but enjoy a life full of rewards and there is a spirit of inquiry and a desire to learn from the great tragedies of life. Creative glimpsed a glimmer that illuminates various areas of life: filming historical films made in beautiful places and happiness is conceived as an access key to a human dimension worthy of much respect. The film gives a sense of time and existence, and there are those who contribute to the prosperity of society beyond the current condition, sex, culture and the evils of the time. The timidity of some actors becomes exasperation of their character and of an unprecedented success: sharp eyes like razor blades reach feelings of joy and glory and all that is shared with all the protagonists of the film. There are those who hails success with great enthusiasm, those who want a viable state that illuminates earthly desires, who embraces harmonious relationships with art and those who face this charming environment with humility and determination, with commitments that are awarded by prestigious awards. The conquest of the role is to everyone's great satisfaction to share with friends and agents: who won the silver ribbon for best actor, who shows the great interest for the adventure, yellow and noir, who often works in film great importance with vanity and arrogance and those who commit a series of dramatic works of great social impact. Mariangela Spalato, Virna Lisi, Monica Vitti are some protagonists of Italian cinema more or less busy and bright. Actresses taxes to the attention of the best directors and screenplay attractive and engaging, are used to film with shades of all kinds and in film productions of great prestige. You may notice the curious and brilliant actors who accept the roles of great force and those who want to be just a free man. If they see others in areas broader cultural and who seeks out the key points of reference in the life and in the speeches of some characters. The American comedies can be an example to follow and praise, and you can see the film in which the individual stands against society more hostile, bigoted and ignorant. Cinematic style is updated more and more and the world society also falls in the dark, when confronted with new problems: the blooming of genres as fires flare up of underwater worlds, the appearances of new media that pave the way consumerism. There are also shades caricatures and new authors who study the psychology of the existence of each one: who distances himself from traditional comedy, those who prefer to wring the hearts of the world and those who are content to embrace the person next door. There are those who follow the Star-traditional system and those who become overwhelmed by the phenomenal, as movie stars and lords of the show to the rescue.

EIGHTH CHAPTER

The magical and sublime lighting Film

In the film world you can meet natural talents of great constructions and incredible myths that have never left any footprints. You may notice satirical aspects that can cheer up the contents of some poignant film or the intimacy of a gripping thriller scary, and there are wild stories as in the case of a plant that can terrorize the entire world. In some thrillers are noted several actions that occur very impressive sequences with pulse-pounding and dangers lurking. There are films to follow for their fascinating pictures and the original characterization of the main characters. There are suspense and anxiety that do, some dramas, thrillers and horror, jewels really intriguing and unusual. You may notice blondes and blackberries world cinema all ready for big business and started to be kissed by success: those who manage to break through in Hollywood and those who are content to shoot some film of little thickness. You can see Hollywood actresses who dress femmes fatales like Sharon Stone in "Basic Instinct", Kim Basinger in "9 weeks and 1/2", Julia Roberts in "Pretty Woman" and Maria Schneider in "Last Tango in Paris ". Films set in the desert or on a roller coaster, held professional and famous falls, integral parts of an urban landscape and elements fable intersect with everyday reality. And 'that's how life responds to the needs of the extraordinary souls purer and thinking. Some artists approach issues that belong to the fear and those who seek creativity in small and fragile things, those pursuing common acts of kindness that mark the days of existence, those who walk on a rainbow and who runs on the edge of a song or a film of thickness. Some people use tools with which you can shape the joy and freedom of individuals and the various species and the person introducing small appendages and pure scenic furnishings to liven up some warm September Glimpsed, among other film events, poor crazed hearts, loving human forces that work from individual to individual, healthy monuments of pride, big projects, big institutions, great emotions, great things, small or medium-sized drops of happiness, gatherings of old stars and amateurs. In the various film tell the first spring sparrows, the various commitments, the sacrifices and the many difficulties of life to digest and know how to manage, the liberation of women, the education of children, the defeat of hatred, of poverty and 'assassination. There is great talent without willpower, but you can see the green and disarming passions which veil the campaign of the artists. There are those who frequently experience the joy of making a kind act and who destroys everything you hold dear in the world, who outer sequences of small kindnesses that are good for the life of every single moment and those facing the fragile beginning of a new life is better. There are films inspired by the big dreams, some people learn to accept the risk of the film system, who plays with the body and eyes, and those who want to prove that the soul most accounts of the thighs. Actresses like Sophia Loren, Gina Lollobrigida, Virna Lisi, Laura Antonelli, Claudia Cardinals, Ornella Muti and Giuliana De Sio, can be considered examples of women with talent and professionalism that go beyond the physical aspect.

CINEMA

Anna Magnani   Brigitte Bardot

Sophia Loren   Stefania Sandrelli

Massimo Troisi   Clark Gable

Mariangela Melato   Virna lisi

Monica Vitti   Giancarlo Giannini

Julia Roberts   Demi Moore

Sharon Stone   Rita Hayworth

Peter O'Toole   Vittorio Gassman

Michelle Pfeiffer   Katharine Hepburn

Ava Gardner   Marlon Brando

Lucia Bosè   Humphrey Bogart

Ingrid Bergman   Charles Chaplin

Montgomery Clift   James Dean

Catherine Deneuve   Alain Delon

Marlene Dietrich   Jane Fonda

Vittorio De Sica   Sean Connery

Greta Garbo   Kirk Douglas

Clint Eastwood   Totò   Judy Garland

Cary Grant   James Dean

Meryl Streep   Audrey Hepburn

Grace Kelly   Marcello Mastroianni

Gary Cooper   Paul Newman

Julia Roberts   Brad Pitt   Rob Lowe

Jude Law   Johnny Depp

Marlon Brando   Jane Fonda

Claudia Cardinale   Giuliana De Sio

Johnny Dorelli   Gregory Peck

John Wayne   Kevin Costner

Robert De Niro   Anna Magnani

Marilyn Monroe   Elizabeth Taylor

Giancarlo Giannini   Franco Nero

Greta Garbo   Totò   Anthony Quinn

Roman Polanski   Gregory Peck

Robert Mitchum   Marcello Mastroianni

Jean Marais   Dean Martin

Steve Mcqueen   Eleonora Giorgi

Giuliano Gemma   Giudy Garland

Michael Douglas   Doris Day

Tony Curtis   Charles Bronson

Giulietta Masina   Barbra Streisand

Frank Sinatra   Sandra Milo

Vittorio De Sica   Carlo Verdone

Robert Redford   Helmut Berger

Kim Basinger   Diego Abatantuono

Roberto Benigni   Walter Chiari

Massimo Troisi Enrico Montesano

Francesco Nuti Nanni Moretti

Renato Pozzetto Luigi Proietti

Laura Antonelli Marisa Allasio

Maurizio Arena Claudia Cardinale

Giuliana De Sio Johnny Dorelli

Sylva Koscina Gina Lollobrigida

Ingrid Bergman Humphrey Bogart

Nino Manfredi Paul Newman

Cary Grant Marlon Brando

Ingrid Bergman Gregory Peck

John Travolta Robin Williams

Robert De Niro Al Pacino

Jack Nicholson Ugo Tognazzi

Alberto Sordi   Roger Moore

Silvana Mangano   Grace Kelly

Bud Spencer & Terence Hill

Matt Dillon   Peppino De Filippo

Charles Chaplin   James Dean

Bette Davis   Catherine Deneuve

Hedwig Fenech   Sabrina Ferilli

Alain Delon   Marlene Dietrich

Roberto Benigni   Paul Newman

Cary Grant   Marlon Brando

Ingrid Bergman   Gregory Peck

John Travolta Paul Walker Cameron Diaz

Robert De Niro Al Pacino Steve McQueen

Johnny Depp   Penelope Cruz

Rock Hudson   Tyrone Power

and many others ...

The notes and pages of 120 years of cinema, colors more 'variety, shapes and content more inviting, open, they browse, read, scrutinize, they love and then close with the hope and the desire to read them again with the same passion that he had initially presented.

Francesco Primerano

Finito di stampare nel mese di Settembre 2015
per conto di Youcanprint *Self - Publishing*